■ THE
ARCHITECTURE
OF
HOPE

The
Architecture
of
Hope

WOOD LAKE

Editor: Mike Schwartzentruber
Proofreader: Dianne Greenslade
Designer: Robert MacDonald
Cover illustration: Douglas MacLeod

Cataloguing in Publication data is available from Library and Archives Canada

ISBN 978-1-77343-174-1

Published by Wood Lake Publishing Inc.
485 Beaver Lake Road, Kelowna, BC, Canada, V4V 1S5
www.woodlake.com I 250.766.2778

Wood Lake Publishing acknowledges the financial support of the Government of Canada.
Wood Lake Publishing acknowledges the financial support of the Province of British Columbia
through the Book Publishing Tax Credit.

Wood Lake Publishing acknowledges that we operate in the unceded territory of the Syilx/
Okanagan People, and we work to support reconciliation and challenge the legacies of
colonialism. The Syilx/Okanagan territory is a diverse and beautiful landscape of deserts
and lakes, alpine forests and endangered grasslands. We honour the ancestral stewardship
of the Syilx/Okanagan People.

GOLD

Printed in Canada
Printing 10 9 8 7 6 5 4 3 2 1

■ TABLE OF CONTENTS

■ **DEDICATION**

To my son, Jack, who is my hope for the future

■ ACKNOWLEDGEMENTS

This book has developed through lunches, coffees, dinners, presentations, debates, and discussions with talented architects, engineers, artists, contractors, and designers from across the country and around the world. In this I also include the students, staff, and faculty at the RAIC Centre for Architecture at Athabasca University. They have all informed, enlightened, and challenged me. Two in particular, however, need to be acknowledged.

Trevor Butler is one of the best "green engineers" working today and is internationally recognized for his work in regenerative design. Climate change wouldn't be a problem if there were more engineers like Trevor.

I first met Robert MacDonald more than 40 years ago when I was a very new architecture student and he was the head of Dreadnaught Press. Over the years, I have been fortunate enough to work with him on projects such as the Banff Publishing Workshops. He is one of the best graphic designers in Canada, but more than that his knowledge, foresight, and commitment to social equity and justice is an inspiration to us all.

We are very fortunate that both of them have chosen to live in the Okanagan Valley.

■ PREFACE

This is a work of "science fiction prototyping," in which a possible future is explored through detailed scenarios. As such, there is no community in the Okanagan Valley named Hope and all of the characters in this book are fictional. Any resemblance to any other persons, or other towns named Hope, living or dead, is unintended and coincidental.

Walking to School

The sun rises early in May in the Okanagan Valley. It climbs above the Monashee Mountains and illuminates the small community of Hope below. As it does so, Hope unfolds much like the flowers that surround it. Shutters and blinds open and solar panels turn themselves to the warming rays of the sun. People emerge, birds sing, and the town comes to life.

Spring is the most hopeful of seasons and every spring bears the promise of life renewed. Why shouldn't our communities mirror the rich potential of the season? Hope is designed to reflect spring in all its glory the entire year-round. The townsite is oriented towards the sun; it follows the natural contours of the geography; and everywhere the native trees, plants, and habitats have not only been preserved but even increased.

The door to one of the houses opens and Paul Kerr and his two children, Carole and Emma, emerge. Alix Lemay, Paul's partner, hugs each of them in turn then hurries back to her home office. She's an architect and she has a large project due later that day.

Paul and the children proceed at a more leisurely pace. They stroll along a path of recycled stone lined with Jack pine, asters, and sagebrush. Malcolm Robinson and Stephen Liu are on their usual bench, but the two elders suspend their ongoing and seemingly endless political debate to call the children by name and to ask them about their latest adventures.

Carole and Emma's school is a five-minute walk from their home, but today it takes them ten minutes. That's okay, because learning is flexible in Hope. Their school is just one of a number of learning buildings scattered throughout Hope. Each one is relatively small and serves between 100 and 200 students. The idea is that everyone gets to know everyone else.

In fact, when they enter, the school most closely resembles organized chaos. Children are running everywhere and even climbing the walls, which are, in fact, designed for climbing. With a coffee shop built right into the lobby of the building, the school is designed to welcome everyone – parents, children, and neighbours. Unlike Malcolm and Stephen, many of the community's elders like to have their morning coffee around the children and enjoy volunteering in the school itself. Play dates are arranged, news is shared, and parenting tips are exchanged.

Paul, however, has work to do and the coffee shop is just a little too noisy. He's a cybersecurity expert and, while he works all over the world, he rarely leaves Hope. The truth is, he lives here precisely because he can walk his children to school.

As he heads for the park, he reflects on his life ten years ago. He was working 12-hour days and most weekends. He was constantly arguing with Alix, as both of them struggled to launch their careers. He was stressed out and anxious at home and at work. He was eating badly and sleeping worse. Then one day, stuck in traffic on his hour-long commute, he listened to a radio interview with Malcolm, one of the founders of the cooperative community movement.

One phrase, in particular, resonated with Paul. Malcolm quoted Chekhov who said, "'Have a look at yourselves and see how bad and dreary your lives are!' The important thing is that people should realize that, for when they do, they will most certainly create another and better life for themselves."[1]

Then Malcolm added, "Our communities are overpriced, poisonous, overcrowded, unhealthy, wasteful energy pigs – not because they *have* to be but because it suits the vested interests that build, operate, and control them."

He continued, "We can now build communities that generate more energy than they need, purify more water than they pollute, grow more food than they consume, recycle more waste than they create, and restore more of the natural environment than they occupy – and we don't need governments, developers, or utility companies to do it for us and empty our pockets in the process."

Paul thought about this all the way home and then checked the movement's website. They were looking for young professionals like Alix and himself. They applied the next day and became part of an experiment in living that is infused with hope for the future.

A New Kind of Park, A New Kind of Community

Paul sits down on a park bench and unfolds his tablet from his knapsack. He doesn't worry about connectivity or security. All of Hope is a giant wireless hotspot with biometric security. The network has already confirmed who he is and Hope has its own telecommunications utility. With customers being charged more and more for less and less, the only sensible response was for communities to begin providing their own services — as many towns and rural areas did in the 1930s when the large telephone companies didn't want to provide service to unprofitable, outlying areas.[2]

A mesh network is simple, inexpensive, and effective to operate. Small, discrete antennas are scattered throughout Hope and provide coverage for the entire neighbourhood. Even devices such as Paul's tablet and phone act as nodes in the network passing wireless signals to the next node.[3]

In addition to the reduced cost, control was another critical issue. With the repeal of laws regarding net neutrality, large telecom companies were free to slow down the traffic of competing vendors. This never happens in Hope.

And that is the compelling and powerful message of the community cooperative movement. We can't rely on our politicians and business leaders to solve our problems or treat us fairly. In fact, we do not need to. We have all the means and methods at hand to solve our own problems by ourselves in a manner that doesn't destroy either us or the planet.

The park that Paul is working in is part of that solution. Like his Wi-Fi, it's part of a "mesh" network of wildlife corridors, wetlands, habitats, and bioswales that demonstrate this new relationship. They're all planted with trees, plants, shrubs, and flowers that are indigenous to the area.[4] He's sitting in the shade of an Oregon oak while the bees buzz around the dandelions and buttercups. There's milkweed for the monarch butterflies and a variety of browse plants for the whitetail deer. When it rains, the landscaped bioswales channel the runoff and help clean the water through a natural process of filtration.

In fact, a mesh network may be the best metaphor for how Hope works. Everything acts as a valued, equal, and interconnected node working in concert with every other node for the mutual benefit of all. It can be parks or Wi-Fi or even people and it works at the scale of houses, streets, neighbourhoods and, increasingly, other communities.

Paul is oblivious to all this as he works. He and his colleagues block a new computer virus, thwart a cyberattack on their network, and close a loophole in their security. The morning flies by and it's soon time for lunch.

He heads back to the school.

The Origins of Hope

■ APRIL 2020

It was a school, or more specifically a daycare playground, that provoked Malcolm to co-found the cooperative community movement. Malcolm trained as an architect but he had made his fortune developing software. It was 2020 and he was staying in a high-class hotel in downtown Toronto. It was late April and all over the city the trees and flowers were in bloom, but when he looked out his hotel room window to the alley below, he saw a fenced and paved courtyard sandwiched between his hotel and an iconic office tower, where the trees were still barren since they received barely any sunlight at all.

To his horror, he watched as the courtyard was flooded with small children and he realized that this was the playground for the daycare centre housed in that tower.[5] He shook his head and thought, "Here, in one of the richest parts of town, in one of the richest cities in Canada, in one of the wealthiest countries in the world – is this *really* the best we can do for our most precious resource? An exercise yard at a prison is larger and more appealing than this."

That night he complained to his partner, Stephen, about what he had seen. Stephen was sympathetic, but as an economist he had to point out, "You can't change anything until you change our value system."

"What do you mean?" Malcolm wanted to know.

"We are surrounded by abundance," Stephen explained, "especially in Canada, but we privilege a value system that is predicated on scarcity."

"I don't understand," said Malcolm.

"Well look – Canada has vast reserves of energy, land, forests, arable land, mineral resources and water and, in fact, by our constitution all those resources belong to the people of Canada."

"So?"

"So the trouble," said Stephen, "is that when those resources are parcelled out to corporations, it's not in their best interest to be generous. In fact, it makes more sense economically to control their distribution and to dole them out piecemeal to create an artificial scarcity and increase their value – or rather, increase what a consumer will pay for them."

"But don't they invest heavily in the infrastructure necessary to make those resources valuable?" asked Malcolm.

"Yes," replied Stephen, "but in many cases they are heavily subsidized by our own tax dollars and, in effect, the wrong people are building the wrong infrastructure for the wrong reasons."

"Huh?"

"Technology has evolved to the point where we don't need megaprojects because we can generate energy, purify water, produce food, and manage waste at the local level. We don't need centralized plants and offshore or distant refineries to do any of those things anymore."

"But doesn't getting the private sector involved cost less?" asked Malcolm.

"The truth is that public-private partnerships don't really cost less and often cost more. In fact, one recent study found that over 17 different projects, these partnerships ended up costing the taxpayers of British Columbia $3.7 billion more than the traditional approach."[6]

"The real problem," continued Stephen, "is that because we have consistently lowered taxes on business[7] and high-income earners over the last 20 years, we can no longer afford even the most basic infrastructure repairs."

"So what do we do?"

"Look at Mondragón," suggested Stephen. And so Malcolm did.

During the Second World War, Malcolm learned, a young priest, Father Arizmendi, was assigned to the town of Arrasate in the Basque area of Spain. In Spanish, the town is called Mondragón. The region had been devastated by the Spanish Civil War and its economy was in ruins. What he did was help the people to help themselves.

In particular, he helped them found a technical school and a credit union. Graduates from the school formed a cooperative workshop financed by the credit union and began producing kerosene stoves. By 2020, the Mondragón Corporation (as they named it) had over 80,000 employees working in over 200 offices around the world and sales of close to 12 billion euros.[8]

"But we don't have a school, a financial institution, or a factory!" protested Malcolm.

"Think outside the bank," suggested Stephen. "Last year, the Canada Mortgage and Housing Corporation (CMHC) had a net income of over $1.4 billion. That's not just revenue, it's profit. Let's see if they could spare a million or two."[9]

"And factories and schools are different animals today. We can tap into Canada's online universities, like Athabasca, for training. And makerspaces are now sufficiently advanced that they could be used to redefine manufacturing."

"So what you're saying is that backed by the CMHC we could manufacture houses in makerspaces to create communities where people could learn, innovate, work, and prosper using online resources," concluded Malcolm.

"Why not?" replied Stephen.

But there was more than that to Mondragón. Father Arizmendi's ten governing principles are its most important asset and independent of any technology. Open admission, democratic organization, sovereignty of labour, capital as an instrument, self-management, pay solidarity, inter-cooperation, social transformation, universal solidarity, and education are nothing less than a blueprint for hope.[10]

Armed with these principles Malcolm and Stephen set to work. While they laid siege to the CMHC, they scoured the country for a suitable site to try out their idea — and they found one in the Okanagan Valley.

In particular, one engineer they spoke with mentioned that due to a peculiarity of its geology, you only need to drill down about a kilometre in the Okanagan to tap into the kind of intense heat that can drive a steam turbine and generate electricity. This is called deep geothermal. A single bore hole could provide an inexhaustible supply of energy to meet all of the community's needs. They decided to drill four.[11]

They sought out potential co-op members via a targeted social media campaign. In very little time they found 500 families who each pledged $200,000 for a home in the new community. In accordance with the principle of open admission, they made sure the first members of the co-op represented a diverse and inclusive group. They also worked with Habitat for Humanity to sponsor and fund an additional ten families.

With $100 million in hand, they asked the CMHC to match it. What clinched the deal was the deep geothermal. Four boreholes would provide far more power than 500 families could use and the rest could be sold for a profit to the surrounding municipalities. And so they bought about a parcel of land about one kilometre wide and two kilometres long above the town of Winfield, British Columbia. Their business plan demonstrated that not only could they pay off their loan from the CMHC in short order, but in a matter of just a few years they would be turning a handsome profit.

"That's what I meant," observed Stephen. "We are surrounded by abundance."

Today Malcolm and Stephen have retired, but they still carry on their debate surrounded by abundance, from that park bench in Hope.

Nourishment Not Just Food

■ **NOON, MAY 2035**

Lunch in Hope is a perfect example of this abundance. School isn't just a place for learning. All of the schools are designed to play a key role in what sociologist Eric Klinenberg called social infrastructure[12] — the libraries, parks, community gardens, and churches where we build a sense of community by creating the connections that make us human. We can design and fund them poorly or well, but whatever we invest in them will, in fact, be returned a thousandfold in the benefits they return to their communities. In Hope, no expense is spared on these facilities because this is where people gather to renew their bonds. Eating together is a critical part of that bonding process. Today, even the community manager, Maya Park, is at the school for lunch.

Alix joins Paul and their children. Even with her deadline looming she makes time to eat with her family because family is valued more than mere work in Hope. Her colleagues on the project not only accept this, they encourage and insist on it.

Every meal becomes a celebration of the bounty of the earth and Hope is a particularly careful steward of that bounty. Food forests, community gardens, and high-tech vertical farms provide all the food the community needs — and then some. The community gains substantial revenue by selling its excess fresh produce at local farmers' markets throughout the Okanagan.

There are nuts and dried berries from last year's harvest, fresh fruits and vegetables grown hydroponically in the vertical farms, and seafood from the aquaponics facility. Not only is all the food grown locally, it is also delicious and new recipes are constantly being shared and improved. Never averse to a new opportunity, the community published *Recipes of Hope*, which soon became a bestseller.

The important thing is that this community controls its own food supply and the quality of that supply. Everyone knows exactly where their food comes from and they can be sure that it is both safe and healthy.

A New Kind of Architecture

Alix hurries back to her home office. Her mind is filled with the work to be done, but as she walks she can't help but reflect on her community and what it has meant to her understanding of architecture.

In her mind, the word itself has undergone a dramatic transformation. Decades ago, the word "architecture" was appropriated by the high-tech world to describe not a physical entity, like a building, but the underlying principles that informed it. So, for example, the architecture of the Internet wasn't about its wires and switches but about the conceptual structures that lie at its heart. The architecture of the Internet was, she realizes, brilliant in its simplicity. It allowed talented amateurs to create radically new business models, applications, and technologies, and in doing so it changed the meaning of architecture.

Some time ago, Alix realized that every complex human system has its own architecture and each of those architectures is driven by its value systems, its policy frameworks, its technologies, and its design principles. Seeing the world through this kind of architectural lens made her look critically at her own profession — and the view wasn't pleasant. Housing was unaffordable; smart buildings were little more than platforms for surveillance; and the policy makers simply couldn't keep up with the dramatic pace of change — let alone protect ordinary people and make the built environment more sustainable and resilient. It was the design principles of contemporary architecture, however, that really gave her pause. Architects seemed more interested in building monuments to themselves than making places to help people solve the problems of the time.

Malcolm had been emphatic about how this had to change: "We need a new kind of architecture — an architecture for life and for hope."

"But can we really create an architecture that embodies something as nebulous and as intangible as hope?" she remembers asking herself. "To map a powerful value such as hope into our material world seems like a contradiction in terms."

As she spent more time in the community, however, she came to realize that it only seemed like a contradiction because we have created a world which squeezes out hope (and other values) in favour of profits. It's difficult, if not impossible, to feel hope unless you are empowered to take control of your own life. The community that Alix and Paul live in provides a scaffold for them to do exactly that.

As she reaches her house, she mulls over the fact that by embodying hope, her community addresses an even bigger issue: "How do we design and build communities that support and help ordinary people to live rich and meaningful lives in harmony with the natural environment and themselves?"

As she slips on her augmented reality headset and rejoins her team, she knows that the answer lies in providing people with a deep under-standing of, and real control over, those environments, but with feedback loops that help them see the actual impact of their activities, and with tools that help them change their behaviour for the better.

"You know," she tells her team, "it's like every building is a school, or at least a learning environment." They're actually designing a new satellite cooperative community further up the Okanagan Valley, to be called Faith, but it too will learn.

"Yes!" quips Lydia, who's logging in from Yellowknife in Canada's Northwest Territories. "It's better to be able to learn than be smart."

This, the team agrees, is true. A smart building never gets any smarter, but a building that learns gets smarter all the time — and learning must be considered the most hopeful of experiences.

It's not, however, that they want buildings to learn by themselves. Over time they want buildings to learn together with their inhabitants and that's what Alix and all of the team members are doing right now. With augmented reality, it's as if they're walking the actual site. They can accurately check solar orientation, views, and sightlines. They're putting the final touches on the design, but they are doing so in concert with their clients (the future inhabitants) and with all of the key stakeholders. That's the way they've been working since the beginning. Everyone takes ownership of the design and the process because their input has been valued and respected from the beginning. This is called an Integrated Design Process or IDP. It's been around for decades, but the design team at Hope has taken it to a whole new level.[13] (The Mondragón principle of democratic organization is embodied and empowered by this process.)

The design team has been working through countless alternatives and rigorously testing them all. As they work in three dimensions, there's a dashboard that tells them how much the proposed design will cost and how much energy, water, and other resources it will need. Over time, the design has become better and better and better — more energy efficient and less expensive. In effect, they have learned how to make a great building.

This process does, however, demand significant access to computing resources and that access is critical to Hope, and hope. Malcolm had been emphatic about how this could happen – he saw it as perhaps the *only* way it could happen. All the cloud computing resources, all the artificial intelligences, and all the robotics that power and operate Hope are owned by the people who inhabit the town.

The people of Hope own their own data. The people of Hope own the tools and technologies that they use. And most important of all, the people of Hope own the profits and revenues that accrue to the use of those tools and technologies.

A future in which large corporations or governments (even democratic ones) control the means of production offers little or no hope (let alone jobs or prosperity) for ordinary people. Measures that benefit the few at the expense of the many are not truly productive for anyone.

To create a different future, however, Malcolm and Stephen added two new principles to Father Arizmendi's original ten principles – re-localization and decentralization – and these, too, are embodied in the cooperative communities.

Water is a perfect example of how this works. Hope does not rely on massive, expensive water filtration plants, pumping stations, transmissions mains, and sewage treatment facilities. Instead, each group of 50 homes acts as its own water utility – collecting its rain water, recycling its grey water for irrigation, and treating its black water with simple, compact reverse osmosis water filtration systems such as those from Zenon Environmental in Oakville, Ontario.[14] Andrew Benedek founded Zenon many years ago based on the idea that our infrastructure design needs to learn from how we developed computers. He observed that we used to have huge, costly mainframes for centralized batch processing, which were only accessible by the acolytes of the IT department. Now we carry inexpensive devices with infinitely more power that fit in the palm of our hands.[15]

In Hope, and in the new community Alix is working on, every neighbourhood is its own micro-utility — or more appropriately, a mesh network — for looking after its own water, energy, communications, and food.[16] Decentralization has empowered Father Arizmendi's principle of self-management not just for labour, but for communities as well. Given the power of this micro-infrastructure, the economies of scale that once helped cities prosper have begun to fade away.

Designing for Hope

Misconceptions, however, about how we should live together have persisted. When Malcolm first imagined Hope, he subscribed to the conventional belief that greater density means a better community.

"I know that's what architects and planners believe," questioned his partner Stephen, "but have you ever seen a study that supports that?"

"Everybody knows that greater density is more sustainable and reduces the cost of infrastructure," countered Malcolm. "And," he added, "everybody knows their neighbours so they get along better."

"Perhaps, but do you have evidence?"

Malcolm was nonplussed but knew he could support his position with lots of research by others, couldn't he?

The more he read, however, the more he became perplexed and then alarmed. There was Corinne Hutt's and Jane Vaizey's 1966 study of the effects on children of playing in greater density.[17] When too many children were placed in the same room, they began to argue (and sometimes fight) after only a few minutes. When Leonard Bickman and his colleagues studied college students in low-, medium-, and high-density residences in 1973, they found the greatest sense of community and generosity in the low-density environments.[18] In the same year, Sheldon Cohen and his colleagues, correlated apartment noise from urban living with diminished reading skills in children.[19]

The animal experiments turned his alarm to horror. Bruce Alexander's experiments in the 1970s suggested that a rat's environment was a more powerful influence on rodent addiction to drugs than the chemistry of the drugs themselves. In effect, the rats only resorted to using drugs such as heroin and cocaine if they were in a high stress environment.[20]

The most frightening of all, however, was John Calhoun's 1958 study of rats stuffed into a series of four interconnected cages. Alpha males established their domains in the two end cages while all hell broke loose in the two middle cages. "Criminal" gangs terrorized the other rats engaging in rape and even cannibalism. He found yet other studies suggesting that langur monkeys will display similar behaviours depending on the density of their environment.[21]

"What have we done?" Malcolm wailed. "This is a nightmare of evidence! And we've known it for decades!

"Stephen, listen to this quote from Bruce Alexander: 'Lack of stable housing in volatile real estate markets dominated by speculators can make settled family and neighbourhood life difficult or impossible for adults, even those [who] experienced little stress early in life. I witness this first-hand amongst young relatives and friends in the insanely inflated real-estate market in Vancouver.'

"Or how about this one," Malcolm continued. "'Existence in a hypocritical, corrupt political system run by politicians who shamelessly serve financial and industrial megacorporations leads to profound apathy in adults.'

"Here's another one: 'Work in a dehumanizing factory system like Foxconn, where my cell phone was probably made, can leave people so empty of meaning that suicide becomes an attractive alternative.'"[22]

"That's precisely why we have to build something better," said Stephen.

The more he thought about it, the more Malcolm realized that the supposed benefits of greater density – reduced costs and greater sustainability – could still be maintained if he adopted a new approach to infrastructure and sustainability. If each neighbourhood served as its own micro-utility company, it would eliminate long runs of pipes, fibre, wires, and pylons to centralized facilities. And if each house generated more energy than it consumed, it wouldn't matter how far apart they were. And if people worked where they lived in a walkable community served by a small fleet of autonomous electric vehicles and drones, then they would no longer need such an expensive system of roads. In the end, Malcolm could see no reason not to provide families with lots as big as a third of an acre. In Hope, there would be lots of space, and green space at that, for everyone.

"But ..." he said hesitantly to Stephen.

"But what?"

"But I don't want this to look like the suburbs. I want something that has a unity and purpose of design, but that still allows larger lots and that can be customized to meet the needs of each and every family," he finally said.

"Surely," said Stephen in exasperation, "in that vast collection of books and magazines that you insist on lugging with us every time we move, there must be *some* kind of precedent for this?"

And of course there was. The city of Bath in the United Kingdom has some of the most elegant streetscapes in the world. From the elliptical Royal Crescent to the circular Circus, these housing developments present a unified public face. Behind that facade, however, each row house has been changed, expanded, and modified over the decades so that each one is now unique. The beauty of Bath was not lost on Malcolm. Why couldn't they do the same in Hope?

Now it was Stephen's turn to protest: "But these houses are jammed tight together."

"That's true," admitted Malcolm. "Our houses will be spaced further apart, but then we'll tie them all together using two elements. Instead of a continuous expanse of Bath stone, we'll have a living wall that runs the length of each set of houses, and we'll create one continuous roof that connects them all and that provides all the utilities, collects the rain water, and acts as the scaffolding for solar panels."

Inspired by Bath, they began to plan in earnest. Learning from the playbook of such living wall artists as Patrick Blanc, Malcolm designed the green facades of the housing clusters, masterpieces of texture and colour, that today change with the seasons. Each one is different and each one uses native plants.

The roofs received a similar treatment. Again Malcolm sought precedents and found them in the art of Sarah Hall, who incorporates photovoltaics into her stained glass windows. He realized that there was no reason solar panels couldn't be objects of beauty as well. This time local artists were engaged to turn these arrays into works of art stretching across the houses. There were intricate Celtic knots, sweeping designs by Northwest Coast artists, and even photomurals. Today, the roofscapes of Hope are widely recognized as artworks unto themselves.

Each house is unique and is constructed from a number of modular units in the form of walls and even rooms that can be swapped out and changed over time as the needs of a family change. Each house, however, still presents a unified front to the world, with carefully arranged front porches and balconies protruding through the living walls.

This has created a unique set of multi-generational houses that are constantly growing or shrinking. Because Hope is now 13 years old, people who came to Hope as teenagers and then moved away are now moving back. Sometimes they buy their own house, but more often they add on to their parents' houses. In other cases, parents whose children may have moved away sell off modules they no longer need. This allows them to age in place – a crucial element for us all as we age. Malcolm had noted the dramatic cognitive decline in elders who were moved from the homes they had occupied for decades and into seniors' residences and he was determined that this wasn't going to happen in Hope. Every effort is made to keep these valued members of the community *in* the community for as long as possible – and being valued *is* critical. The veteran from the Canadian Armed Forces is often asked to talk of her experiences in Kandahar. The retired business person mentors young entrepreneurs.

As Malcolm put it, "Helping to educate our youth is a reward for a life worth sharing. There can be no greater joy than sharing your experiences with hungry minds and then watching them exceed anything and everything you have ever accomplished."

In addition to welcoming elders as volunteers at the schools and libraries, their opinions and experience are actively sought on all critical decisions and activities affecting the community. In return, there's a whole cadre of young people whose job it is to check in on the elders, who also enjoy priority seating at events and first call on the autonomous vehicles.

With this approach, Hope is organized into ten groups of 50 homes apiece that include a wide range of ages and family groupings.[23] Across the landscape, these groups are arranged into a variety of different forms. There are ellipses, circles, and squares borrowed from Bath, but there are also undulating curves and complex geometries. Each cluster is different and responds to its own part of the landscape. The lots tend to be narrower in the front but wider towards the rear. This allows a tighter public face while providing bigger back yards which radiate outward from the homes. Collectively this creates large public areas in front of the homes — like the park that Paul was working in — which are a key part of Hope's social infrastructure.

Integrated with these housing clusters are other types of buildings — vertical farms, schools, libraries, and coffee shops — which help to animate the public spaces. Across the back of the properties is a four-metre-wide urban garden that runs in a continuous strip around each cluster. Some people like to tend their own gardens, but others utilize the services of urban farmers who tend multiple plots all over Hope. Being an urban farmer is considered an important and prestigious position in the community. This group also tends the vertical farms like the one in the cluster where Alix and Paul live.

Growing Up

Of all the structures in Hope, Malcolm is proudest of the vertical farms. For him, they are a visible symbol of how the cooperative community movement has re-localized food production and ensured the quality, safety, and control of its own food supply. Inside these towers with their south facing glass fronts, hydroponics and aquaponics are combined to grow all manner of fruits and vegetables, and to raise fish, crabs, and other seafood in a circular metabolism where each form of food helps to fertilize and replenish the other.

Inside the farms, the floors rotate to make the maximum use of all available sunlight and from their roofs swarms of drones constantly arrive to pick up parcels of fresh produce, which they then deliver to homes throughout the community using special hatches built into the roofscape of the housing.

The farms were one of the key elements in securing approval for the zoning for Hope. Hope is situated in what is called the ALR or Agricultural Land Reserve, which is intended to preserve the farmland in the province of British Columbia. Stephen and Malcolm were able to prove to the satisfaction of the local council, however, that if Hope was built, the property would actually produce significantly more food than in its current usage as pastureland. Not to mention the fact that, all over the world, people were reducing their consumption of red meat for both the health and environmental benefits.

Once again, the actual numbers Stephen produced had Malcolm scratching his head.

"You're saying that acre for acre, growing crops on the land generates 17 times more food calories than using the same land for livestock?"[24]

"Yup," said Stephen.

"And you're saying that compared to traditional crops in a field, a vertical farm uses 200 times less water and has a crop yield that is 20 times greater, while reducing the distance those crops are transported by a factor of 40?"[25]

"Yup."

"So the yield per square metre per year from our vertical farms would be more than 300 times that of the current use of the land as pasture!?"

"Yup."

"That means that by building just four, four-storey vertical farms, 20 metres by 20 metres, we could generate as much food as the entire two-square kilometre parcel does now?"

"Yup."

"This isn't a difficult calculation to make," said Malcolm, "so what I really don't understand is why the hell we're not doing this already?"

"Because, sadly, despite the well-known dangers of climate change, humans don't like to change their ways unless they absolutely have to," replied Stephen.

In the end, they built six vertical farms and with the urban gardens and the food forests they doubled the production of the land and realized significant environmental benefits. These are the very real advantages of decentralizing and re-localizing food production – and again this resource is self-managed by the community. While robots guided by artificial intelligence conduct much of the vertical farming, the humans who work with that technology are highly skilled partners in the operations of these structures.

Manufacturing Hope

■ MIDAFTERNOON, MAY 2035

Alix's team is about to prove the value of Hope's people-centric control of production. Everyone is now pleased with the design and they take one more walk through the virtual community they've created. Now it's time to begin building it.

The design is sent to Hope's maker network. It's another example of a mesh network in action. The network is composed of an interconnected system of 3D printers, laser cutters, and robotics guided by artificial intelligence. You'd miss the point, however, if you thought it was just about technology. Embedded in this network is the accumulated design knowledge of the community. More than artificial intelligence (AI) and robotics, the principles of modularity, universal access, negative waste, and healthy and regenerative living guide the design. At the same time, if much of the means of production can be localized and distributed, as it is here, then it no longer needs to be centralized.

Archana Montgomery manages Hope's manufacturing network and she's been expecting this order. In fact, she was a key part of the design team.

"It's hard to believe," she reflects as she sets the "build" in motion, "that even at the start of the 21st century we were still making homes the same way they made Gothic cathedrals – one brick at a time and one piece of wood nailed to another and another and another. It was as if the industrial revolution never happened to architecture."

Here the process goes directly from file to factory — or rather factories. The new town will be built utilizing a mesh of printers and cutters distributed throughout Hope. Every home, office, school and library has some kind of maker device, large or small, and jobs of various kinds will be scheduled across off hours. The printer in someone's kitchen, for example, may start printing draw pulls in the middle of the night. The larger equipment, which can create walls and floors 10 metres long and 5 metres high is located in the centre of town, but by distributing the work it can be done better, faster, and for less cost.

One local company the people of Hope learned from was Spider Agile Technology, which operated at the north end of Kelowna, about 20 kilometres south of Hope.[26] Spider created plug-and-play electrical components that simply snap together to provide all the wiring a building needed.

The designers of Hope took this idea to its logical conclusion and made plumbing fixtures, communications components, cupboards, counters, shelving, windows, and doors that fit together easily and quickly. This is such a simple and common sense idea that it is almost amazing that it has taken over ten thousand years of building to implement it. Last year, for example, Archana designed a new window latch that's easier to operate if you have arthritis or another ailment that makes gripping things difficult. The new design simply screws into the old fitting and it's done. What works with window latches, is also applied to walls, roofs, stairs, and floors.

It was Malcolm's mantra that "Walls work with rooms which work with homes which work with neighbourhoods which work with cities which work with countries which work with planets — in one seamless mesh of shared, healthy, and sustainable resources for the greater good of everyone." This is the expression of the principle of universal solidarity and of how Hope itself works in a global network of cooperative ventures.

"Today, if you act locally, then you're acting globally whether you like it or not!" is how Malcolm sums it up.

Modular and universal design, however, is only part of the story. Malcolm was adamant that this community had to be more than sustainable. He liked to quote the American architect, William McDonough, who once said, "Being less bad, is not being good."[27] Malcolm took this even further and said, "When the world is going to Hell, it does no good to be neutral."

He pushed the architects and engineers to improve the environment of Hope, and became a tireless advocate for regenerative design. Everything in the community is designed to not just have a positive impact on the natural world, but to act as a force of continuous improvement. As he said time and time again, "The big idea is that we could restore rather than destroy; we could produce rather than consume; and we could purify rather than pollute – not just the Earth but our bodies and minds as well."

That's why there are far more trees on the land now than ever before. That's why there is far more flora and fauna. That's why the water is cleaner. That's why the food is fresher. That's why the air is better. And that's why the people are healthier and happier.

"It's not about technology," Archana reminds herself as she watches the process begin. "It's about using human-centric technologies wisely.

"Still," she chuckles to herself, "some of this stuff is pretty sweet."

She particularly likes the walls. These weren't designed as barriers but as adjustable filters. They can let in the sun or keep it out. Sometimes fresh air flows in and sometimes stale air flows out, as if they were breathing. They let the rain in to irrigate the living walls, but keep it out of the interior. The rain is also combined with sunlight and carbon dioxide to create synthetic photosynthesis right in the wall, which generates oxygen and hydrogen that are stored in fuel cells to produce energy while at the same time reducing greenhouse gases.

In 2015, the noted Canadian architect and visionary Philip Beesley founded the Living Architecture Systems Group by posing the question, "Can architecture integrate living functions?"[28]

In the buildings of Hope, each window, wall, door, and fixture is alive with sensors. They report on, monitor, and strive to improve their own behaviours. Over time this feedback helps every element of a house become better.

"In Hope," Archana thinks, "Beesley's question has been answered with a resounding yes!"

All of this was made possible by the material revolution at the dawn of the new millennium. The intricate, honeycombed structure of the walls is 3D printed in nanocrystalline cellulose — an extraordinarily strong material made from plant fibres.[29] Not only is it natural and non-toxic, but it is an anti-oxidant and actually good to be around. This inner web of NCC is specifically designed to resist all of the forces that act on a building but using a minimal amount of material. Inside the honeycomb is an aerogel, a super lightweight insulator, also derived from NCC.[30] The result is a ten-metre panel that can be easily carried by two people, but which can resist any earthquake, hurricane, or fire. Moreover, due to the unique properties of NCC, the panels can act as reflective filters that can be "tuned" to reflect or admit light, making them ideal for smart windows.

This feature also allows the facades of all the buildings in Hope to be wrapped in ever-changing explosions of colour. This serves no useful function, but it is a constant delight to inhabitants and visitors alike.

As Archana checks on the giant printers that have begun squirting out the walls, she waves to the other people working in the makerspace.

"It's true," she observes, "that there aren't as many manufacturing jobs in Canada as there used to be — but at least here those jobs are in Canada, and even better, all the equipment here is owned by, and produces profits for, the people of Hope."

And profitable it is. They now run 24 hours a day, seven days a week pumping out home after home for a global market.

Nor is this meaningless, mindless, automated labour. Archana remembers researching her mother's family tree. In the small village in Yorkshire that she came from, in centuries gone by, all the jobs were highly skilled — harness makers, blacksmiths, carpenters, crofters, and cobblers. But when labour is in service to capital (rather than the other way around), the meaning of work and its associated skills are often replaced with the repetitive, mind-numbing tasks of the assembly line or the service industry. This may maximize profits and efficiency but it deadens the soul.

That's why Father Arizmendi included both the "sovereignty of labour," and "capital as an instrument" as key principles of Mondragón. In Hope and in other co-ops, capital is a resource used by people to make better products, services and, critically, jobs — not something to make more money for those who control it.

Yes, there are people in Hope who have to clear up the dishes at the school after lunch, but that's not all they do. Negative waste is a key component of regenerative design and every scrap of garbage is now valuable. Those who work in the community's waste management program are passionate not just about re-using, but about finding the most innovative uses for everything that was once sent to the landfill. Using online resources, mentors, and co-op programs, even entry-level positions are trained in material science, chemistry, and advanced manufacturing. Tonight some of the 3D printers will be using a slurry developed by Hope and made out of biocomposites, compost, and garbage. This is the principle of self-management in action.

Learning to Play, Playing to Learn

Self-management infuses every aspect of life in Hope and, in truth, it changes the nature of work. Archana slips on a pair of glasses that present "the build" in augmented reality. Reaching into the empty air she connects needs to resources using the elegant, graphic user interface.

"This is more like a video game than a job," she reflects.

In fact, Malcolm and Stephen learned a lot from video games, so much so that they dared to change one of Father Arizmendi's principles from "education" to "playing to learn." Learning is an activity that by its very nature expresses hope for the future, so why shouldn't it be fun as well?

"All mammals are hardwired to learn through play," noted Malcolm. "Just watch a kitten or a puppy – or a kid who knows more Latin than a scholar because the names of dinosaurs are in Latin. Some animals, like the bonobos, never stop playing and learning.[31] Our school system, on the other hand, still seems to be able to squeeze the fun of learning out of our children by age ten. We complain that Canadian companies aren't innovative enough but the very subjects that foster creativity – like art and music – are always the first things cut in a budget crisis!

"It's like a quote I once read," added Stephen. "'We don't stop playing because we grow old; we grow old because we stop playing.' We have to do a better job. It's not about education, it's about learning, and learning through play – not just at school but through your entire career and your entire life. Imagine if work was fun. Imagine if work was indistinguishable from play — then we would have a society that is both creative and innovative."

And so Archana innovates by "playing" with the system that will print the new town. She laughs out loud when she finesses a particularly difficult aspect of the project.

Early on in the process, Malcolm and Stephen engaged some of Canada's finest learning designers to help craft the experience of Hope. The best learning is immersive they were told. Immersive learning occurs when you are totally absorbed by the experience at hand and so they set about creating a community of immersive learning environments.

They were clear, however, that these environments didn't need to be technology-driven. The naturally occurring forest that is part of the community is one of the best immersive learning environments of all. The Japanese concept of *Shinrin-yoku* or "forest-bathing" captures the idea that just immersing yourself in the woods is good for the mind, body, and soul. In Hope, adults and children alike regularly comb through the woods appreciating its treasures, from the giant 200-year-old Jack pines to the intricate web of sap, lichen, and moss that regulates the forest.

Inspired by that forest, they commissioned other immersive learning environments. For "geometry bathing," they created a room that wraps the visitor in areas, volumes, proportions, progressions, and conics. Light boxes, material halls, and design hives soon followed. Like the vertical farms, these are spread throughout the community and integrated with the housing. The light box, with its changing colours, projections, and effects, is part of Alix and Paul's group and is a favourite of their children. At the same time, they realized that many of the key components of Hope from the vertical farms to the makerspaces were also places for immersive learning. Children are always welcome – not just for field trips but for hands-on activities and, for the older ones, internships. Tomorrow, for example, Archana has set aside some of her resources so that senior high school students can help middle school students 3D print their designs.

Malcolm and Stephen weren't anti-technology, they just used it when appropriate. They licenced the historical environments of ancient Egypt and Greece that form part of the Assassin's Creed series from video game maker Ubisoft.[32] With the violence removed, these are beautiful and extremely accurate reconstructions of life in those distant civilizations. Some of the profits from Hope were also used to help the people of Haida Gwaii build a virtual reconstruction of Sgang Gwaay, with its extraordinary architecture.

One of the most powerful immersive learning environments, however, is the virtual model that was created for Hope itself. A digital twin of the physical community was created and it behaves just as the real one does. Visitors can walk the streets and sit in the park. They can explore the public buildings and check in on the makerspaces and the vertical farms. They can even check the energy output of the deep geothermal, and the water quality in the bioswales.

Malcolm and Stephen took this one step further, however. They created another virtual version of Hope that is distinct and separate from the digital twin. This they christened the "crash test model"; with it, anyone can try out scenarios for the future.[33] What if there were five bore holes? What if they doubled the insulation in all the walls? What if they doubled the population? What about an earthquake? A forest fire? Or a global depression?

Crash test models have now become a key component in Hope's learning repertoire and they're constantly commissioning new ones for chemistry, biology, physics, and math. Ingredients explode, habitats implode, cars drive into walls, and connected pendulums swing wildly — all without anyone being hurt.

Augmented reality or AR is used to take learning even further. Focus your tablet on a flower in the woods and find out what its name is. Go online and you can watch badgers in their den, ospreys in their nest, and deer sipping water at the pond.

The most radical — and controversial — innovation had to do with artificial intelligence. While companies and organizations all around the world were replacing humans with AI and robotics, Hope created synergies between all three.

Paul was at the forefront of this. "We can't ignore these developments but we can make them work for us," he argued. In fact, he pushed for the idea that everyone who wanted one should have their own AI that would belong to them and them alone, and that every child entering the school system would be assigned an AI that would learn along with them. He has since come to regret this decision as his daughter Emma is going through a "cat phase" and talks endlessly about what she and her AI, who she recently renamed Fluffy, did today. Nonetheless, Emma and Fluffy will grow and learn together and eventually enter the workforce as an invaluable combination of human creativity and computational power.[34]

This is exactly what's happening right now on the floor of the makerspace. The laser sintering machine that prints metal parts has broken down and four intelligences, two human and two artificial, are working to fix it. With glasses on and the AR app switched on, Archana and David, a technician, are consulting with Lisa and Vive, their respective AIs. This time it's Archana, playing a hunch, who finds the faulty circuit first; but it's Vive, one of the AIs, that controls the robot that delicately slips the new component into place.

Running Hope

Unlike Alix, community manager Maya Park lingers after lunch to enjoy a coffee and talk to the other residents. When the weather is nice, however, as it is today, she conducts most of the community's business from the flourishing garden she maintains in her backyard. She has no need for an office.

Managing a community that includes mesh networks, microgrids, vertical farms, artificial intelligences, robotics, and a robust manufacturing industry, is not for the faint of heart, but Maya relishes the challenge.

She's the highest paid employee in Hope, but in accordance with the laws of the co-op she only earns ten times more than the lowest paid employee. This is the principle of pay solidarity. She could earn much more elsewhere – and outside companies have made those offers.

Long ago, however, she realized it's not about the money. She was a single parent with two small daughters when she first arrived in Hope. Not only has the community provided them with a superb education, it has allowed her to be there with her children as they grew up. During the early years she was often at the school to have lunch with them. She also took advantage of Hope's mentorship program and quickly rose through the ranks.

But there's more than that. As Stephen often said, "You can make money or you can make a difference." Maya knows her work makes a difference.

And, she thinks as she prunes a lilac tree between calls, where else could I work amidst bumble bees, hummingbirds, and the occasional squirrel? Or hold meetings on my front porch?

"Why," she wonders as she spreads compost in her garden, "did people insist on sitting in traffic for hours each day to work in an office when technology had evolved to the point where it was far more productive to work from home? What possible advantage is there in working in an office?

She does have a team, but they too work from their homes or gardens. They're all within walking distance as well, so many meetings *do* occur on her front porch.

At the same time, Hope is not run like a traditional municipality or corporation. In accordance with the principle of democratic organization, the community often uses a method of direct democracy, where all the inhabitants are invited to vote on key issues ranging from dental plans to co-op fees. These debates can be fractious, but every voice is heard and every vote counts.

For there to be real hope for everyone, she reminds herself, every voice *does* need to be heard and every vote really does count.

In too many past elections, political parties courted votes until election day and then ignored people and catered to powerful lobby groups for the next four years. No wonder people grew disenchanted with the system.

Like Alix, Maya soon learned to use a modified Integrated Design Process to ensure that voices were not just heard but listened to and acted upon.

She remembers in particular what Malcolm told her when she was first elected to her position. "At the heart of hope is the belief in our endless potential. Everyone in this town must believe that whatever their circumstances today — good or bad — they are empowered, even required, to improve and make them better not just for themselves but for everyone.

"If you actually believe in your own endless potential, then everything becomes a hopeful experiment conducted with a heartfelt belief in the future," he concluded.

Some days this can seem an impossible challenge, and not every experiment — hopeful or not — has been successful, but Maya has managed Hope for the past seven years and has watched it grow and prosper. Every four years an election is held, but she remains a popular figure in the community — particularly after the Great Fire of 2029.

One of the reasons she is so good at her job is that she never stops learning. Remembering the fire, she shakes her head and decides to run the crash test model that mimics that emergency. She sets the degree of difficulty to high and grits her teeth. High winds, a prolonged drought, and a rockslide that blocked the highway through the valley make this simulation devilishly hard to beat. An hour later, she's sweating but successful. "At least the highway wasn't blocked in 2029," she says.

The Content Co-op

All of these digital learning tools — AR apps, crash test models, simulations, and immersive learning environments — may be the most valuable assets of Hope, which is why Stephen insisted they be given away. More precisely, he said that they must be shared in the spirit of universal solidarity, as open educational resources or OERs.

"If knowledge is power," Stephen intoned, "then learning is even more powerful because it is the best way to create new knowledge. Let's democratize learning by making it easily accessible and affordable." Today, anyone can use or download these OERs from the community's website.

It was Paul, however, who suggested a critical tweak to this approach. One day, after he had been living in Hope for about two years, he saw Stephen sitting on his bench.

"Um…" he began badly. "You know the OERs? It's great that they're free, but they could also make us substantial revenue."

As an economist, Stephen was fascinated by what appeared to be a contradiction.

"In the summer of 2015, the Canadian rapper Drake was one of the most popular performers on the planet," Paul explained. "His mixtape *If You're Reading This It's Too Late* debuted at number one on the Billboard 200. During August of that year, if you had searched for Drake on Google and then clicked on an ad that accompanied the search result, the advertiser would have paid Google somewhere in the neighbourhood of $16. How much of that revenue did Drake receive?"

Stephen knew the answer, but he let Paul continue.

"Absolutely nothing; but pay-per-click (PPC) ads like that propelled Google to a record $19.5 billion U.S. of net income in 2016!"[35]

Paul explained, somewhat unnecessarily: "Google uses a two-sided matching market, micro-auction system in which the winner of the auction pays a price that is actually based on the next highest bid. This serves to encourage higher bids because it reduces the penalty for over-bidding. This micro-auction occurs with each and every search query."

"I do know how Google makes its money," commented Stephen, "but sadly not every artist is as popular as Drake."

"I know," said Paul. "That's where it really gets interesting. Even for genres like rhythm and blues, the average bid price is still about the same as the cost of a song on iTunes."

"That's interesting, but what does this have to do with our OERs?"

"Well," said Paul, "We can continue to offer them for free, but a small ad could run while they're being downloaded based on the same two-sided matching market, micro-auction system."

Stephen thought about this. The fact was that there was plenty of money being generated from digital content in 2027, but almost all of it was still going to two companies – Google and Facebook – who then garnered some 85% of all new ad revenues on the Internet. Again, none of this was shared with the artists or performers whose names and activities generated much of the traffic to those online applications.

"Why stop at OERs?" he asked Paul. "Why couldn't we make all of our content free? Our designs, our artistic creations, our software, everything?"

"I don't see why not," stammered Paul. "Once anything is digitized, it's only a matter of time before it's pirated, but this approach might actually harness the power of piracy to aid the creators."

"We'd need a critical mass of content to make this work," mused Stephen.

"There are an awful lot of artists and musicians out there who don't get gallery shows, publishing deals, or recording contracts," said Paul, who was a failed musician himself. "Just the chance to have a showcase for their work, let alone make a small profit, would mean a lot to them."

"Exactly!" exclaimed Stephen, "But it would also do something even more important!"

"It would?"

"Absolutely! You see we live in two different value systems – one of market exchange where things cost money, and one of social exchange based on our relationships with our family and friends where we help each other without ever thinking about being compensated. Next Thanksgiving, try paying your in-laws for the dinner they prepared and you'll see what I mean."[36]

Paul laughed out loud at this.

"By doing this," Stephen concluded, "we could move content creation from market exchange to social exchange and enrich the world (and artists) immeasurably. When can you start work on this?"

And so the Content Co-op was born. Paul's work of genius was to embed the micro-auction so deeply in the content that it wasn't worth removing. Even when uploaded to torrent sites (the mainstay of online piracy), the ads still ran and the revenue still went to the content creator.

Alix's work of genius was to suggest that the website could move beyond a flat two-dimensional environment to become a three-dimensional, immersive learning environment itself.

"Like an Expo," she suggested. And with that she and her team started designing a concert hall where you could download music; a theatre where you could download movies; a gallery for the visual arts; a library for texts; and then, in quick succession, an observatory, laboratory, planetarium, and museum. These were also integrated with the physical learning environments. Soon people were curating the digital content creating exhibitions, collections, and even performances.

With this approach they soon reached the critical mass that Stephen needed and, while the revenues were modest, 85% of them went to the content creators, which made the site very popular.

When the CBC came calling, they knew they had a success on their hands. The Canadian Broadcasting Corporation had failed miserably at monetizing its vast archives of content, but with Paul and Alix's approach they realized they had stumbled upon a winning formula and asked to load their archive into the Content Co-op.

Getting around Hope

Ignoring evidence is something that humans are very good at – whether it's online content or climate change. Transportation is another example. When he started planning Hope, Malcolm dredged up an old issue of *The Atlantic Monthly* magazine that he had saved since 1988. It was a special issue on Los Angeles, but the reason he saved it was for a single paragraph:

The Southern California Association of Governments recently commissioned a computer model of greater Los Angeles transportation in the year 2010, which examined the effect of measures like double-decking freeways, building more freeways, expanding mass transit, and imposing traffic-management plans. According to the model, everything that could feasibly be done would be only a gesture toward meaningful relief of the expected congestion except one thing – moving employment closer to housing and vice versa. This solved the congestion problem.[37]

In other words, all the things we do to solve traffic problems don't actually work and the one solution that does work, living where you work, we chose to ignore.

In Hope, Malcolm insisted, the major form of transportation would be at the end of your legs and the community is therefore designed for walking. What makes this possible is the fact that almost everyone works where it is convenient for them – at home, in the coffee shop, or on a park bench. For longer journeys, bikes are the favoured form of transportation. Living where you work and working where you live have made traffic congestion a moot point.

In fact, Hope is designed to be walked and bicycled. The pathways have been carefully designed to work up and down the sloping hillside – crisscrossing it in the manner of donkey trails that ensure that no path is too steep. Moreover, the planners took the concept of "desire paths" to a whole new level. Desire paths are those direct routes that people take – often cutting across lawns and grass – to reach where they want to go. Not only did the planners create direct routes, they also made those routes attractive and comfortable with landscaping, shade, and places to sit. These pathways are also a critical part of the health of the community. Malcolm and Stephen created an app that maps routes of 10,000 steps so inhabitants can get their daily exercise. The two elders can often be seen practising what they preach, as they stroll across the community on a daily basis, walking sticks in hand.

Sometimes, however, walking and cycling just won't do, so they also put in place a system of electric autonomous vehicles of various kinds that, not surprisingly, function as a mesh network. A new sofa may arrive from the makerspace by electric truck; someone with mobility problems may be picked up by a minivan; your fruits and vegetables may arrive by a drone; another drone picks up the drawer pulls your 3D printer printed last night; and a much larger drone may fly you to nearby Vernon.

Like many aspects of Hope, these vehicles also serve multiple purposes. Because each of these electric vehicles is essentially a mobile battery, they are also a critical part of Hope's micro-grid. With the need to move power around in the community micro-grid, these cars became part of a V2G (Vehicle to Grid) solution. When needed, they roll or fly to the desired location and connect to a building, event, or activity to provide it with the power it needs. Conversely, when they're low on power, they will recharge on buildings or other locations with excess power. It's not unusual to see a swarm of drones resting on the roofs of Hope soaking up energy from solar panels.

Sometimes when the central makerspace is running overtime, as it is tonight, Archana will commandeer a dozen or more vehicles to drive themselves to the makerspace, plug themselves in and add some more juice to the process.

It was improved battery performance that made energy storage affordable and transformed the possibilities of the grid. When the price of storing a kilowatt-hour of energy dropped below $150 in 2025, Stephen and Malcolm realized that community-sized batteries could be an essential part of their power strategy. Today, the makerspace mesh churns out large scale batteries that can handle all the storage needs of a small hotel.

This is a peculiarity of the way that the community operates. Even though Hope could easily serve all its own requirements with its deep geothermal system, in accordance with the principles of self-management, localization and decentralization, everyone is encouraged to manage their own energy. Every household tries to generate its own power using the renewable sources (such as wind and solar) that are built into its fabric, and many earn additional credits by selling their local excess power back into Hope's micro-grid.

People are also encouraged to manage their personal energy and health. The app and the walking paths that Malcolm and Stephen created can also log your daily activities and, depending on your age and other factors, you receive similar credits every time you exercise.

At the same time, they worried that rewarding certain behaviours smacked of behaviourism and so they made all such programs voluntary. People can opt out at any time. Moreover, they also applied the principle of self-management to personal data. Everyone in Hope has the right to decide if and when any data is collected about them and they own any and all data that is collected. This right to your own data is a fundamental part of Hope's charter. To ensure that no one felt coerced, they insisted that there be no rewards or credits for sharing data. Many do share their data, however, because data is the real currency of the modern world and sharing it helps Hope run better. Paul's job is to make sure that that data stays protected and secure.

Now, however, his working day is over. The drones have delivered a fresh batch of produce and to celebrate the success of Alix's latest project, Paul makes a family favourite – a seafood paella. The scallops, prawns, and crab have all been grown locally, as has the saffron, basil, and thyme – not to mention the wild rice. They eat quickly, however, because tonight is the annual DroneFest and they want to get good seats at the amphitheatre.

DroneFest

■ **TWILIGHT MAY 2035**

When all is said and done, living should be fun. There is, of course, no reason why hope can't be fun. In fact, it's difficult to imagine that if you actually had social equity, a fair distribution of wealth, and meaningful work that life wouldn't be fun.

That's where cultural expression comes in. The Content Co-op is one such vehicle for cultural expression, as are the roofscapes and facades of the housing, but there are special events as well and DroneFest is one of the best.

The event is held at twilight on the second Tuesday in May in the amphitheatre, which is a naturally occurring depression that has become an outdoor stage for the community. It can hold all the inhabitants of Hope plus a few hundred more, but each year the festival attracts more and more visitors so Alix, Paul, and their children have to scramble to get a good spot.

DroneFest was inspired by the extraordinary work of Raffaello D'Andrea, who time and time again in the 2010s demonstrated the creative potential of this technology.[38] Tonight, there'll be mobile light shows that pulsate across the darkening sky; drones with speakers controlled by musical instruments that fling music over the site; drones that interact with acrobats somersaulting through space; drones that dance to DJs; and the always popular People's Choice performance in which the audience members use their smart phones to control the drones.

Alix and Paul hold their collective breath as the last performance begins. It's called Flying Architecture and Alix helped with the design and Paul with the programming.

There's a low rumble as the woofers kick in and begin to pulse their bass notes. Semi-transparent columns of glowing fabric begin to rise from the ground.

A spotlight picks out a theremin in the centre of the stage. A theremin is a strange electronic instrument usually played by the proximity of your hands to two antennae – one that controls pitch and the other that controls volume. It produced the wobbling electronic sound on the Beach Boys' "Good Vibrations." Here, however, it is played by two small drones. The delicacy and precision of their movements plays the instrument in a way it has never been played before. Moreover, the rising columns begin to move and oscillate with the sounds produced by the instrument.

More drone-flown architectural elements appear. Flying cornices define a roofline while hopping drones bounce a vaulted ceiling into place. The entire edifice shakes in the twilight sky and begins to dance.

Alix and Paul turn to each other and smile. It's going well and they know what's coming. An instant later, the projector-carrying drones are turned on and a whole new dimension is added to the performance. They had carefully studied the work of Refik Anadol who, two decades ago, had revolutionized the art of projection mapping.[39] Advances in computer graphics had allowed artists to accurately map shapes and textures onto irregular surfaces and then animate them to create extraordinary illusions of depth and perception. That's precisely what the audience is seeing now as the architecture seems to warp, slump, and melt into impossible shapes, forms and colours.

The music and the architecture rise to a crescendo then abruptly stop to leave the silence and darkness that signal the end of DroneFest. The audience is on its feet delivering a standing ovation.

Maya Park seeks out Alix and Paul to congratulate them for she knows the part they played in the performance. They walk together out of the amphitheatre, which is located at the northern edge of Hope adjacent to the wetland. As they look across to the aspens on the far side of the wetland, all of them remember the Great Fire.

The Great Fire

■ **2 A.M., AUGUST 2029**

When her phone rang in the middle of the night, Maya knew it wasn't going to be good. That summer the Okanagan Valley was a tinder box, with high temperatures and little rain. A carelessly tossed cigarette high up on Oyama Lake Road was all it took to set to the forest ablaze and now it was headed directly towards Hope. To make matters worse, Hope was all that stood between the fire and the town of Winfield.

Only a year or two into her first term as community manager, Maya was still growing into the job and she often felt that Malcolm and Stephen were always looking over her shoulder. She squared her shoulders and decided that now was her time to show her worth.

She logged into Hope's emergency simulator and selected the forest fire crash test model. A hundred times she had selected the "simulation" option. Tonight she clicked the "Actual" one. The system asked for confirmation and she gave it.

All over Hope, phones rang and alarms sounded. She dressed quickly but carefully and headed to the command centre headquarter in the makerspace. She didn't run but she walked with purpose and, as she walked through the community she had helped build, she knew that Hope was worth fighting for.

Lights were being turned on all over the area. Autonomous vehicles were on the move and overhead drones flew by. In her head, she recited her own personal mantra to calm herself: "Let hope, and Hope, give me courage," to calm herself. As others joined her walking toward the command centre, she made sure she projected the confidence she didn't feel.

Everyone who needed to be, and those who weren't part of the firefighting team, were being evacuated. Families were already heading out, but Alix and Paul didn't have children yet, so they both hurried to the command centre.

"No one's panicking," thought Maya. "That's a good sign."

When she arrived, Malcolm and Stephen were already there. "Great," Maya thought. "Just what I need!" She saw Malcolm open his mouth to start telling her what to do, but Stephen put a hand on his arm and simply said, "She's got a job to do and she knows exactly how to do it."

"Think of this as just another simulation," she told the team when they had all arrived. "We done this dozens of times and we're properly prepared. Everyone knows what to do, so let's do it."

They were prepared. Hope is always more resilient when it is prepared. In fact, fighting this fire started years ago when the community was first designed. Noting the ability of aspen trees to resist burning, Hope is surrounded by a protective ring of these trees.[40] Within that ring, there had been a six-metre firebreak and a natural wetland, which had been expanded and connected to reinforce this second line of defence.[41] Moreover, every year, brush and biomass were cleared throughout the area to minimize the danger of fire, and reused for a wide variety of purposes including making nanocrystalline cellulose. This year the community had run a controlled burn in May and, in anticipation of this possibility, Maya had made sure they had stockpiled water and fire retardant. She had checked the stocks yesterday and they had what they needed.

But this fire was a bad one.

"It's already a Rank 4," the local fire marshal told her by phone. "The flame front is spreading fast, with a forward rate of spread (FROS) of six klicks an hour, and we've already seen some aerial bursts. The water bombers will be here soon, but they won't be much good until daylight. We'll launch a parallel attack along its western flank. If you can hold the centre we may be able to deflect it to the east and back away from the town.[42]

"But…" and here he paused, "if it hits Rank 5, we all have to evacuate."

"I understand," she replied, "but I want your permission to initiate a broadcast burn just beyond our boundaries."

He considered this: "We may lose some homes, but we'll lose more if we don't," he said finally.

"Broadcast burn," she told her team. A swarm of drones carrying large bundles of slash took off almost immediately. Slash is forest waste and Hope had stockpiled a large amount of it when they cleared the brush that year. The slash was spread, or broadcast, by air over the area beyond the aspens, and then another drone with a driptorch shot out a stream of what was essentially napalm to ignite the slash and create a backburn, which would burn back towards the approaching fire and deprive it of fuel.

Paul led the drone team. All of them had logged hundreds of hours flying drones and, with screens and joysticks, they could deliver anything, anywhere. Soon a new ring of fire burned towards the approaching blaze.

"Fuel, weather, and topography," thought Maya reciting the elements of the wildfire triangle to herself. They had done everything they could to reduce the fuel or combustible materials that kept the fire alive; they had built the necessary firebreaks and other defences; but there wasn't anything they could do about the weather. A strong wind from the north was doing nothing to help.

In the absence of the airtankers and helicopters, Hope's drones dumped fire retardant onto the blaze even though it was still kilometres away. Each of the large drones could carry 4,000 litres of fire retardant. Maya coordinated their efforts with the fire marshall. It helped, but they couldn't stop what was now an inferno.

Two hours later, the fire was still bearing down on them and, according to data from the drones, it had reached a FROS of seven kilometres per hour. In another hour it would hit Hope. The vehicles had completed the evacuation and now, equipped with a strange assortment of attachments, they moved into the wetland. Some hauled water tanks and others had fire hoses mounted on their roofs. Others, called hedgehogs, bristled with cylindrical canisters of fire retardant that could be shot over half a kilometre into the heart of the fire. Alix's team directed the vehicles and they were quickly maneuvered into their assigned positions.

With the vehicles in place, Maya gave the order to flood the wetland. A number of water tanks opened and water cascaded down the slope.

With the wetland flooded and the back fire burning, they had done everything they could. As the sun came up, the fire marshall phoned again.

"We need to pull back our fire line. It's getting too big and there are reports of candling. Candling occurs when a tree bursts into flames and burns from the ground up. It is a sign of an aggressive Rank 5 fire.

Maya hung up and spoke to her team. "The fire marshall says it's getting serious. We've simulated this kind of fire many times over and we know we can stop it but... I won't hold it against anyone who wants to leave."

Alix looked at Paul and stayed put. So did everyone else. Malcolm and Stephen brewed a pot of fresh coffee.

"Then let's hit this bastard with everything we've got," said Maya.

As a blood red sun rose above the mountains covered in smoke, they fired the hedgehogs. Each one held 30 canisters of fire retardant. With infrared sensors and proximity fuses, they were designed to seek out the hottest spots of the blaze and burst just above it. They fired salvo after salvo into the heart of the fire. It slowed the fire, but didn't stop it.

As it grew closer, the drones took off again. They soaked the aspens until they shimmered dark red with fire retardant through the smoke. The fire hit the back burn and slowed some more. The wind kept it moving, but it had been pushed back to the ground by the back burn.

With greater water content and less of the chemical makeup that makes a pine tree so combustible, aspens are a natural means of slowing down a fire, but would they be enough?

The fire hit the ring of aspens. They smoked and charred, but they did not ignite. Here and there the surface fire pushed through them and into the wetland. If the fire stayed low and out of the crowns of the trees, Hope might have a chance.

"Engage the water cannons," ordered Maya.

The hoses mounted on the autonomous vehicles swung into action and doused the flames wherever they appeared. Drones kept pouring on the fire retardant. Paul cursed as one flew out of control and crashed into the fire.

A massive gust of wind blew a wall of flames into the wetland and engulfed a vehicle. Someone gasped. The other vehicles smothered the burning wreck with water.

Then they heard the water bombers coming in. While it's really the ground crews who put out the fires, that didn't stop the team in the command centre from cheering.

Another tongue of flame pushed through the trees but it wasn't as strong as the last one. A few more followed but with less and less intensity. The wind began to die down. By 7 a.m. they felt they had won. They remained on station and vigilant but by 10 a.m. they knew they had beaten the fire.

By stopping it, they had not only saved Hope but the houses and towns further down the valley. For some time afterwards, Maya was treated like a hero wherever she went and she won the next election hands down.

Regeneration

Aspen trees thrive after a forest fire and six years later they were growing nicely as Maya, Paul and Alix strolled by after DroneFest.

"Regeneration," murmured Maya, mouthing one of Malcolm's favourite terms.

"Of the mind, the body, the soul, and the environment," she continued, almost hearing Stephen expanding on the idea.

Spring isn't a singular event but rather an annual occurrence. Early on, Malcolm and Stephen realized that hope should also be a recurring aspect of everyone's life.

As Stephen has often said, "The community that is truly hopeful will provide social equity, a fair distribution of wealth, an infrastructure for regeneration, and a blossoming of cultural expression."[43]

In their later years, Malcolm and Stephen had devoted themselves to thinking about that infrastructure and how it could regenerate people across multiple generations.

"Regeneration can and *should* occur at any age," insisted Malcolm as they hiked across Hope a few years after the fire. They were discussing the problem of Canada's ageing population and the fact that they weren't getting any younger themselves.

Wait!" Stephen asked. "Do you really believe that you can regenerate your mind and think new thoughts even at our age?"

"Exactly!" said Malcolm as they reached the far side of the wetlands.

"And that you can regenerate your body and even learn new skills *at our age*?" Stephen emphasized the last three words.

"Precisely!"

"But do you really believe we can regenerate our souls and become someone new, *even at our age*?" Stephen almost shouted the last four words.

"I believe we can, and we *must*," intoned Malcolm, "*because* it is only by regenerating our bodies, minds, and souls that we can regenerate the planet. As Gandhi said, 'If we could change ourselves, the tendencies in the world would also change.'[44]

"But it's not a static thing," Malcolm added. "True regeneration is a process of continuous improvement. Imagine if the mere act of living made you and the world around you better. Why can't we do that?"

"But as we grow older," wondered Stephen looking at Malcolm, "can we really still improve? Can us old dogs learn new tricks?"

"I believe we can, and we must if we are to keep our mental health. This idea that you can't learn new things in old age is nonsense."

"But how?" Stephen wanted to know as a light breeze blew through the pines.

"Deliberate practice," Malcolm replied. "I believe it is the secret to learning *anything*. Focus all your attention on what you're doing. Don't allow distractions. Start slowly, performing the correct motions and sequences and then repeat, again and again and again."

"That sounds too simple," said Stephen skeptically.

"Well, it *is* simple, extremely simple in fact, but it's also devilishly difficult to do," acknowledged Malcolm. "Imagine that your brain is like a landscape. When water flows across a landscape it creates ruts and rivulets and creeks. That's what happens when the experiences of your life flow across your brain. They carve into and shape your memory. The more they're repeated the more powerful the memories become."

"Alright then," said Stephen. "Tomorrow you and I start training, and designing, to test your premise."

Malcolm sighed. "I really should be more careful about what I say."

They approached Alix the next morning as she walked the children to daycare.

The physical component proved the easiest to implement. Again, they found examples in Klinenberg's book *Palaces for the People*. A Finnish company, Lappset, boasted of combining "three generations" with a "seniors sport area" of low-impact equipment, such as balance beams.[45]

The first time he tried the balance beam Stephen was dubious, but when he stuck with it — a critical part of deliberate practice — he became adept at it. Balance in seniors is key to preventing devastating falls and soon elders throughout the community were lining up for their turn.

Of course, Malcolm and Stephen added some variations of their own. The equipment was nestled into their network of parks and they deliberately mixed up the equipment that was for different generations. They also updated their exercise app to include these new activities as well. And they borrowed from a design group called Science Play to include one of their play planetariums, which is a climbable dome with the holes cut into its covering that represent the night sky.[46]

Regenerating the mind was not as easy, but when Alix and her team started digging what they found was surprising.

"Fred Gage's work from the 1990s suggests that even adult mice can grow new brain cells — neurogenesis," said Alix, adding, "*if* they live in a stimulating environment; and they grow them in the hippocampus."[47]

"Hopefully, we've got that part nailed," allowed Malcolm.

"Then a few years later," Alix continued, "Eleanor Maguire noticed that London cab drivers had a greatly enlarged right hippocampus compared to the general population, and that its size was proportional to the number of years they had been driving cab."[48]

"So the knowledge changed the physiology of their brains?" asked Stephen referring to the intense navigational test that London cab drivers must face to get their licence.

"Apparently," said Alix. "But Maguire also studied contestants in memory contests and found that nine out of ten used something called places and images."[49]

"I know this one!" declared Malcolm. "Loci and Imagines!"

"Yessss," said Alix. "That is its Latin name."

"Alright," said Stephen. "How does it work?"

"You take a place you know well and then you make up symbolic images of the thing you want to remember. Like a Big Mac to remember Sir John A. Macdonald, Canada's first prime minister. Then in your mind you place your images in a sequence of distinct locations around your place. So, for example, you would place the image of the Big Mac on the windowsill in the middle of your living room; then you would imagine the Mackenzie River (for our second prime minister, Alexander Mackenzie) flowing out of the corner of your living room next to the window; and so on."

"And this actually works?" asked Stephen.

"Not only does it work," replied Alix, "but Maguire found it was lighting up the hippocampus of those who practised it."

"Why do you keep mentioning the hippocampus?" Malcolm wanted to know.

"Because that part of the brain plays a crucial role in making new memories and in learning. Most critical of all, the hippocampus starts to shrink after the age of 30 and when its cells start to die it's often a sign of Alzheimer's disease."

"Okay," pondered Malcolm, "Let me see if I've got this straight. If we stimulate the hippocampus using the places and images technique, could we actually create new brain cells in that part of the brain and maybe, just maybe, delay the onset of Alzheimer's?"[50]

"Do you have any idea what that might mean economically?" asked Stephen. "Last year, the cost to our health care system and caregiver costs was over $16 billion!"[51]

"So what do we do?" asked Stephen and Malcolm almost in unison.

"That's why I asked Paul to join us," smiled Alix.

"Augmented reality," he began. "We create a series of memory challenges of increasing difficulty that use the locations – benches, tree stumps, climbing equipment, art works – of our desire paths. Pointing your phone at one of those locations shows the image of the thing to be remembered. It could be prime ministers, or queen and kings, or the elements of the periodic table, or pi to 100 digits."

"Brilliant!" said Malcolm. "We combine mental and physical exercise!"

"We've absolutely got to give this one away!" declared Stephen. "It's simply too valuable for us to try to control it."

"Agreed!" they all said.

Changing souls, however, was the most difficult of all. They expanded their design group to include Maya as well.

"I once walked El Camino de Santiago de Compostela in Spain. It made me think that the soul is more of a journey rather a destination," she noted.

"That's why Gothic cathedrals, like Chartres, often had a labyrinth or maze cut into their floor," added Alix

"Maybe we could create a similar journey…," began Malcolm.

"With AR?" Paul suggested.

"Perhaps this is an instance when you neither need nor *want* technology," Maya said gently.

"What do you mean?" he asked, crestfallen.

"It seems to me that to truly regenerate your soul you need to see what you already have and begin to appreciate it," she replied.

It was hard to argue with this.

"Maybe all you have to do is move a bench, reframe a view, plant a tree, or narrow a path to make walking through Hope a more spiritual journey. Let's help everyone here see the positive aspects of their lives and let's provide plenty of places and opportunities for people to meditate mindfully on the beauty of their existence."

And so they set about tweaking Hope to do exactly that. They couldn't resist, however, in creating one or two labyrinths set into the landscape and, in a nod to Paul, they 3D printed handheld "finger labyrinths" that fit in the palm of your hand and allowed those with limited mobility to experience a spiritual journey as well.

Nightfall

Sleep is also a critical part of regeneration. It's hard to be hopeful if you haven't had a good night's sleep so Hope is designed to help people get the rest they need.

In particular, it's quiet. Electric vehicles are virtually silent and by nightfall most of them are safely docked and recharging their batteries.

Alix and Paul put their children to bed and then enjoy a few moments of meditation together on their back porch. It's been a busy day and this ritual helps them relax. They share a pot of chamomile tea and Alix traces a finger labyrinth as she meditates because it helps her focus.

Not for the first time, Paul reflects on the beauty of Hope's aural environment; frogs and owls are the loudest sounds they hear.

It's also dark. Street lighting is kept to a minimum and it's carefully shaded and focused towards the ground to avoid light pollution so the stars shine brightly in the night sky. By the soft light of the crescent moon they watch as the shadows of the deer move across their backyard.

"It's not that Hope 'gives' us hope directly," muses Alix, who has been thinking about this all day. "It's that it provides us with a support structure so that we can create full, meaningful, and hopeful lives together for ourselves, our children, and our neighbours."

And with that they headed off to bed hand-in-hand, as the lights dimmed, shutters closed, and Hope folded into itself to rest and regenerate.

■ NOTES

1. I first read this quote in another book called *In the Face of Fear: On Laughing All the Way toward Wisdom* by Walter G. Moss (Kelowna: Wood Lake Publishing, 2019), 33. It's taken from a letter Chekhov wrote to Alexander Tikhonov and the full quote is as follows. "All I wanted was to say honestly to people: 'Have a look at yourselves and see how bad and dreary your lives are!' The important thing is that people should realize that, for when they do, they will most certainly create another and better life for themselves. I will not live to see it, but I know that it will be quite different, quite unlike our present life. And so long as this different life does not exist, I shall go on saying to people again and again: 'Please, understand that your life is bad and dreary!'" (http://www.notable-quotes.com/c/chekhov_anton.html)

2. Derek Slater and Tim Wu, "Homes with Tails: What if You Could Own Your Internet Connection?" New America Foundation, Wireless Future Program, 3–4. See https://scholarship.law.columbia.edu/faculty_scholarship/1565

3. For more on mesh network see https://www.cbc.ca/news/technology/wifi-nyc-mesh-new-york-city-1.4617106

4. The scientist and conservationist Diana Beresford-Kroeger has created a website called Call of the Forest that includes an app to find what trees are native to your area. See http://calloftheforest.ca/plant-a-tree. She believes that if each of us planted one native tree per year for six years we could solve global warming.

5. I am sad to say that I saw this myself a couple of years ago.

6. This is also true. See "Public-Private Partnerships in British Columbia," Columbia Institute (2018), 4. See https://ameqenligne.com/news_pdf/pdf_docs__20180612070622_1_12.PDF

7. The corporate tax rate in Canada was 38% in 1986 and 15% in 2012. See Richard M. Bird and Thomas A. Wilson, "The Corporate Income Tax in Canada: Does Its Past Foretell Its Future?" *The School of Public Policy, SPP Research Papers*, University of Calgary 9, no. 39 (2016): 5.

8. See https://www.mondragon-corporation.com/en/about-us/economic-and-financial-indicators/highlights/

9. Canada Mortgage and Housing Corporation, *Building a Place Called Home: Annual Report 2018*, 8. https://eppdscrmssa01.blob.core.windows.net/cmhcprodcontainer/sf/project/cmhc/aboutus/corporate%20reporting/annual-report/cmhc-annual-report-2018.pdf

10. See https://www.mondragon-corporation.com/en/co-operative-experience/our-principles/

11. Trevor Butler, a Kelowna-based engineer, told me about this. Using essentially the same skills and equipment as used by the oil and gas industry, he estimates that 4 bore holes could supply all of Kelowna's energy needs in perpetuity. See also https://www.cangea.ca/britishcolumbiageothermal.html

12. Eric Klinenberg, *Palaces for the People: How Social Infrastructure Can Help Fight Inequality, Polarization, and the Decline of Civic Life* (New York: Crown Publishing Group, 2018). This is a critically important book that suggest we don't need megaprojects or signature buildings but rather smaller, community-based places of all kinds. This is what architecture should be about. Thank you to Robert MacDonald for sharing this with me.

13. IDP should be the only way to design buildings. For more about how it works see Busby Perkins + Will Stantec Consulting, *Roadmap for the Integrated Design Process*, 2007. http://www.greenspacencr.org/events/IDProadmap.pdf

14. Sadly, after being bought by GE in 2006, Zenon's operations were moved to Hungary in 2010. Nonetheless, a Zenon Z-Box S18 can clean the water of up to 1,200 homes a day for a price of about $200,000 using reverse osmosis. See https://www.youtube.com/watch?v=uW138pqVjhO

15. This is from an interview Benedeck gave to CBC Radio shortly after winning the inaugural Lee Kuan Yew Water Prize in 2008.

16. Nafeez Ahmed, "Decentralized Microgridding Can Provide 90% of a Neighborhood's Energy Needs, Study Finds," *Motherboard, Tech by Vice* (2018) https://tinyurl.com/vlsdw89

17. Corinne Hutt and M. Jane Vaizey, "Differential Effects of Group Density on Social Behaviour," *Nature* 209 (1966): 1371–1372.

18. Leonard Bickman, Alan Teger, Thomasina Gabriele, et al., "Dormitory Density and Helping Behavior," *Environment and Behavior* 5, no. 4 (1973): 465–490.

19. Sheldon Cohen, David C. Glass, and Jerome E. Singer, "Apartment noise, auditory discrimination, and reading ability in children," *Journal of Experimental Social Psychology* 9, no.5 (1973): 407–422.

20. Bruce Alexander's work has been ignored and maligned because it doesn't fit with conventional wisdom about addiction. You can find more about Rat Park at his website https://www.brucekalexander.com/articles-speeches/rat-park

21. John B. Calhoun, "Population density and social pathology," *Scientific American* 206, no. 2 (1963): 139–148. I first read about this experiment in an article called "The Violent Way" in the September 11, 1970 issue of *Life* magazine. It is truly frightening. You can find this article at https://tinyurl.com/uvzkzbe

22. All these quotes are from Alexander's article on "Addiction, Environmental Crisis, and Global Capitalism," which can be found at https://www.brucekalexander.com/articles-speeches/ecological-issues/addiction,-environmental-crisis,-and-global-capitalism

23. In his book *Grooming, Gossip and the Evolution of Language* (Boston: Harvard University Press, 1998), anthropologist Robin Dunbar suggests that primates self-organize into groups based on their cognitive abilities. For humans, the size of these groups is 150 individuals. This is known as the Dunbar Number. If each house has on average 3 people, then each housing cluster will have about the same number of inhabitants as the Dunbar Number.

24. This graphic of land use is very instructive: https://ourworldindata.org/land-use Note that of the habitable land on Earth, only 1% is used for urban living. I have used this information to calculate the food caloric yield from pasture land versus crops.

25. These figures come from https://www.eitfood.eu/blog/post/is-vertical-farming-really-sustainable

26. Their facility is still in operation but Spider was bought by DIRTT Environmental Solutions in 2008.

27. William McDonough is one of the pioneers of regenerative design. For more about this quote, see https://ecorner.stanford.edu/videos/being-less-bad-is-not-being-good

28. Beesley is a visionary and the LASG is defining the future of architecture. See http://livingarchitecturesystems.com/ for some of the incredible things they are creating.

29. This really is a miraculous material. See https://www.nrcan.gc.ca/our-natural-resources/forests-forestry/forest-industry-trade/forest-products-applications/cellulose-nanocrystals/13349

30. Another incredible material. See https://en.wikipedia.org/wiki/Aerogel#Applications

31. Bonobos are without a doubt the most interesting primate of all. See https://www.wnyc.org/story/what-can-bonobos-teach-us-about-play/

32. These spinoffs from the videogames are beautiful. See https://assassinscreed.ubisoft.com/game/en-gb/news-updates/332957/discovery-tour-by-assassin-s-creed-ancient-egypt and https://www.youtube.com/watch?v=tX8xgPV03IE

33. I first heard this term several years ago from Klaas Rodenburg, President of the Alberta Council of Technologies Society.

34. For more on this idea, see a piece I wrote with Dr. Vive Kumar called "Learning Scenarios: Affective Intelligence" at http://architecture.athabascau.ca/docs/AI_booklet.pdf

35. In 2015, as part of my research I tracked these bid prices for a year. It is incredible that artists of all kinds are not getting the revenues they deserve from the online world.

36. I first read about this in Dan Ariely's book *Predictably Irrational: The Hidden Forces that Shape Our Decisions* (New York: HarperCollins, 2008. The dinner example appears on p. 67.

37. C. Lockwood and C. Leinberger, "Los Angeles Comes of Age," *The Atlantic Monthly*, January 1988, 54.

38. Visit Verity Studios at https://veritystudios.com/ and prepare to be amazed.

39. Refik Anadol is another visionary designer. See http://refikanadol.com/

40. While these qualities of aspen trees are important, it is heartbreaking to read that the government of British Columbia is systematically poisoning these trees because they are not as valuable as those that produce softwood lumber. If you ever doubted that we are the architects of our own misfortune, see https://www.cbc.ca/news/canada/british-columbia/it-blows-my-mind-how-b-c-destroys-a-key-natural-wildfire-defence-every-year-1.4907358

41. For more on the role of wetlands see http://theconversation.com/how-to-fight-wildfires-and-climate-change-with-wetlands-117356

42. For more about wildfire behaviour see https://www2.gov.bc.ca/gov/content/safety/wildfire-status/about-bcws/wildfire-response/fire-characteristics/behaviour

43. The International Living Future Institute takes these ideas even further. See https://living-future.org/wp-content/uploads/2016/12/Living-Building-Challenge-3.0-Standard.pdf

44. Apparently Gandhi never said, "Be the change you wish to see in the world." For a full account of the history of this quote, see https://www.nytimes.com/2011/08/30/opinion/falser-words-were-never-spoken.html

45. See https://www.lappset.com/

46. See http://www.scienceplay.co.uk/

47. Fred Gage, "Brain Repair Yourself," *Scientific American* 289, no. 3 (2002): 46–53. This is groundbreaking research. If only we had the sense to pay attention to it!

48. See https://www.scientificamerican.com/article/london-taxi-memory/

49. See Eleanor Maguire, Elizabeth Valentine, John Wilding, and Narinder Kapur, "Routes to remembering: the brains behind superior memory," *Nature Neuroscience* 6, no. 1 (January, 2003): 90–95.

50. This idea is pure speculation and needs to be tested.

51. The Alzheimer Society of Canada predicts that this will be true by 2031. See https://alzheimer.ca/en/Home/Get-involved/Advocacy/Latest-info-stats

Over the last 30 years, Dr. Douglas MacLeod has been creating visionary projects that have transformed the arts, architecture, and education. From pioneering work in virtual reality at the Banff Centre to eduSourceCanada — the country's largest e-learning initiative to date — MacLeod has led the work that defines our future. A registered architect, he is currently the Chair of the Centre for Architecture at Athabasca University, an online program that has quickly grown to be one of the largest and most innovative in the world. Now in his latest work he weaves together architecture, technology, and economics into a compelling vision of how we can live together in the future.

For Everything a Season

■ THE WISDOM OF TRADITIONAL VALUES IN TURBULENT TIMES
WARREN JOHNSON

For Everything a Season reignites the sacred flame. Warren Johnson urges us to recommit to faith, while maintaining our reason. Guided by traditional principles embedded in the great teachings of the New and Old Testaments, he offers a hopeful path to creating a modern eco-system where every individual consumes and creates in balance with the sacred whole. In this way, we do away with excess, make reparations for our past, and ultimately lead a happier, healthier life.

ISBN 978-1-77343-166-6

96 pages, 4.25" x 6.25" paperback, $12.95

Creative Aging

■ STORIES FROM THE PAGES OF THE JOURNAL "SAGE-ING"
CAROLYN COWAN & KAREN CLOSE

Creative Aging is a powerful social and cultural movement that is stirring the imaginations of communities and people everywhere. Often called Sage-ing, it takes many forms: academic, social, and personal. Sage-ing is about seeking – satisfying inner gnawing and transforming it to knowing and action. Aging can be alchemy when one allows the realization that to know thyself and contribute that knowing to our culture is indeed one of life's highest purposes. That knowing brings the gratitude, grace, and integrity that a life deserves. The creative journey into self is a strong aid to health and wellbeing for the individual and to culture.

ISBN 978-1-77064-790-9
320 pages, 6" x 9" paperback, $24.95

Activist Alphabet

■ DONNA SINCLAIR

Donna Sinclair's book *Activist Alphabet* is an effort to figure out why and how activists fall passionately in love with a cause, a watershed, or a planet and its people. It's a primer, or an alphabet, on how to stay strong enough to keep putting that love into action, over and over. As author Donna Sinclair explains, it is particularly aimed at people of faith, because love, we say, is what we are about, even though it makes us terribly vulnerable to grief and loss. Good and evil, we say, is what we are about, even though that calls us to study and learn and intervene, trying to protect. Trying to find hope. Trying to see where God fits and lifts in the current chaos.

ISBN 978-1-77343-154-3
176 pages, 5.5" x 8.5" paperback, $19.95

WOOD LAKE

IMAGINING, LIVING, AND TELLING THE FAITH STORY.

WOOD LAKE IS THE FAITH STORY COMPANY.

It has told
- the story of the seasons of the earth, the people of God, and the place and purpose of faith in the world;
- the story of the faith journey, from birth to death;
- the story of Jesus and the churches that carry his message.

Wood Lake has been telling stories for more than 35 years. During that time, it has given form and substance to the words, songs, pictures, and ideas of hundreds of storytellers.

Those stories have taken a multitude of forms – parables, poems, drawings, prayers, epiphanies, songs, books, paintings, hymns, curricula – all driven by a common mission of serving those on the faith journey.

WOOD LAKE PUBLISHING INC.
485 Beaver Lake Road, Kelowna, BC, Canada V4V 1S5
250.766.2778

www.woodlake.com